MARY
Jesus' Mother

written by

Melissa C. Downey

Susan L. Lingo

illustrated by

Roy Green

STANDARD PUBLISHING
Cincinnati, Ohio

Library of Congress Number 92-61781

ISBN 0-7847-0032-X

The Standard Publishing Company, Cincinnati, Ohio.
A Division of Standex International Corporation.

00 99 98 97 96 95 94 93   5 4 3 2 1

Mary: God's Servant Girl

Matthew 1:18–25; 2:1–23; Luke 1:26–56; 2:1–52

"Greetings! The Lord has blessed you and is with you."

The angel's voice sounded all around Mary. Her young, dark eyes peered over the pale blue veil. Fearfully, she focused on the mighty angel, her heart trembling as he gently spoke:

"Don't be afraid, Mary, because God is pleased with you. You will give birth to a son, and you will name Him Jesus. He will be great, and people will call Him the Son of the Most High. The Lord God will give Him the throne of David. . . . His kingdom will never end. The Holy Spirit will come upon you, and the power of the Most High will cover you. The baby will be holy. He will be called the Son of God. . . . With God all things are possible!"

Mary humbly answered, "I am the servant girl of the Lord. Let this happen to me as you say."

Mary's heart sang with joy. "My soul praises the Lord! My heart is happy because God is my Savior. I am not important, but God has shown His care for me, His servant girl. From now on, all people will say I am blessed because the Powerful One has done great things for me. His name is holy."

Mary was engaged to be married to Joseph, a good man, a carpenter from Nazareth. As soon as he learned she was to give birth to the special baby, the Son of God, he and Mary were married. Some time after that, they learned they would have to go to Bethlehem to be counted for taxes.

Bethlehem was the hometown of their ancestor David. The trip was very long and hard for Mary because it was almost time for the baby to be born. When they finally arrived in Bethlehem, the little city was packed with people to be counted. All the inns were full, so Joseph found shelter for Mary in a stable. In the soft hay, Mary gave birth to Jesus. She wrapped Him snugly and laid Him in the manger to sleep.

The stars of heaven have never shone more brightly! The angels have never sung so sweetly! The heavens were filled with rejoicing. Angels appeared to some shepherds and told them of Jesus and how to find Him. The shepherds came with great joy and found Mary, Joseph and Jesus. They told Mary and Joseph what the angels had said about the baby Jesus. Mary remembered the angel's words to her

months before. Now, here was the miracle God had promised. Here was the Son of God for her to care for and to love. Mary cherished these things in her heart and thought about them often.

When Jesus was eight days old, Mary and Joseph took Him to the temple in the city of Jerusalem. In the temple, Simeon and Anna had prayed each day, awaiting the coming of God's Son into the world. When Simeon and Anna saw the baby Jesus, they knew in their hearts that He was the Son of God, the one for whom they had prayed so long. They thanked God and praised Him for Jesus.

Simeon said to Mary, "Many in Israel will fall and many will rise because of this child. He will be a sign from God that many people will not accept . . . And the things that will happen will make your heart sad, too."

Mary wondered at what Simeon said about Jesus. How could Jesus make her heart sad? Mary held these things in her heart.

Some Wisemen traveled the long way from the east to see and worship baby Jesus. Following a special star, they came to Bethlehem bringing kingly gifts for the baby who would fill David's throne. When they saw Jesus, they worshiped Him. Mary was awed. Soon after the Wisemen left, the angel of the Lord appeared to Joseph and warned him that the evil king Herod planned to kill Jesus.

"Get up! Take the child and His mother and escape to Egypt. Herod will start looking for the child to kill Him. Stay in Egypt until I tell you to return."

Joseph took Mary and Jesus to Egypt. After Herod died, the angel of the Lord came again to Joseph and said, "Get up! Take the child and His mother and go to Israel. The people who were trying to kill the child are now dead." So they returned to Israel and settled in the town of Nazareth.

A very special time of celebration for Israel was the feast of Passover. Each year they celebrated how God had saved them from being slaves in Egypt. Joseph always journeyed to Jerusalem for the feast days. When Jesus became twelve years old, He too was allowed to make the journey. The roads to Jerusalem were crowded with people. Thousands of people entered the city for the feast days. The city of Jerusalem hustled and bustled with activity! When the celebration came to an end, the people started their long journey home. Mary and Joseph traveled for a whole day before they realized that Jesus was not with the other young people in the group. Jesus had stayed behind. Mary was afraid that something bad had happened to Jesus. Hurriedly, they returned to the city to look for Jesus. They searched the city for three days. Mary was frantic with worry. Finally, they found Him in the temple. "Son, why did you do this to us? Your father and I have been worried! We've been looking for you," Mary said to Jesus.

But Jesus replied, "Why did you have to look for me? You should have known that I must be where my Father's work is!" Mary did not understand the meaning of what He said, but she thought about and remembered all that happened.

and were married. They were until the Roman told all the to go their hometowns to counted. The wanted the to give him $ for taxes, so and left 4 . was expecting GOD'S holy , Jesus, so she rode on the back of a and grew very weary.

When and came to , they could find no room 2 stay. kept believing in GOD's love, and soon they found a where were kept, so they stayed there. The shone brightly as Mary's was born! the Light of the , was born! The of heaven sang, and hid the joy of the Lord in her ! loved . He was more precious than and sweeter than the sweetest . And the child grew and was strong in spirit and the grace of GOD was upon Him.

When was 12 years old, and took Him to Jerusalem to the Feast of Passover. When they started for home, and could find ! For 3 days they looked 4 Him. Finally, they found in the , teaching the men of GOD! How they were to find in His Father's ! raised with love in her . She knew GOD would always love and keep His on His beloved !

Who Was That?

Unscramble the names of the characters from the story. Then draw a line from the name of the character to the picture of the character.

seusJ __ __ __ __ __   ●   ●

nmoeSi __ __ __ __ __ __   ●   ●

yMra __ __ __ __   ●   ●

lgeAn __ __ __ __ __   ●   ●

Seehhprd __ __ __ __ __ __ __ __   ●   ●

Using the names from above, identify the one who said:

______________ "Greetings! The Lord has blessed you and is with you." Luke 1:28

______________ "I am the servant girl of the Lord." Luke 1:38

______________ "Many in Israel will fall and many will rise because of this child." Luke 2:34

______________ "We've been looking for you." Luke 2:48

______________ "You should have known that I must be where my Father's work is." Luke 2:49

Raise PRAISE!

Mary knew in her heart how deeply God had blessed her by choosing her to be the mother of Jesus, God's holy Son. She lived, loved, and worshiped with a thankful heart for the wondrous gifts God had given!

Fit the words from the following Scripture verse into the boxes below. Then use the numbered letters to complete Mary's praise to God!

"For the Mighty One has done great things for me—holy is his name."
Luke 1:49 (NIV)

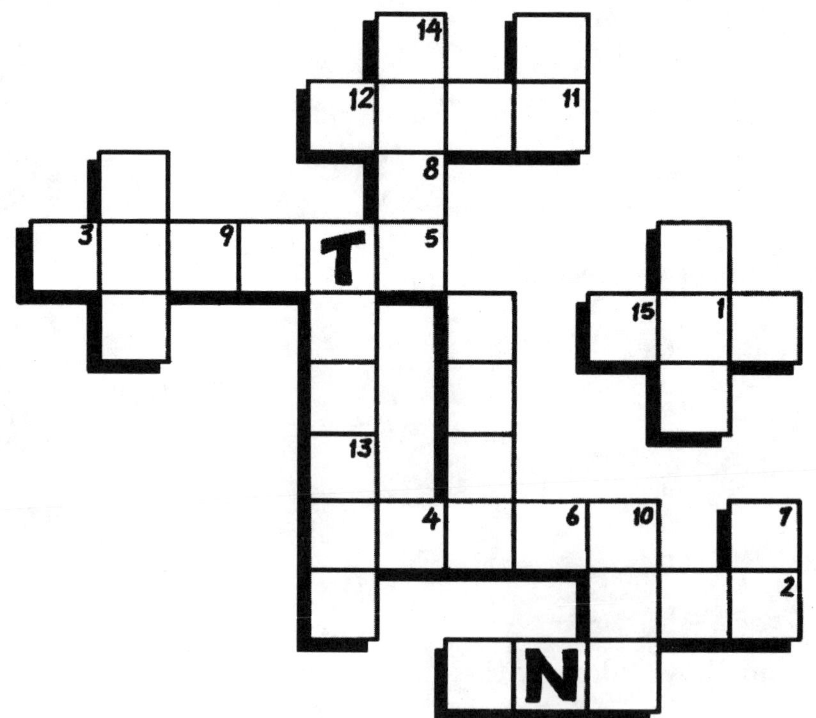

Serve Up Some Giving

Stacks of dishes piled in the sink. Good thing it's not **your** night to do the dishes! Then Mother comes home from work. She is late and tired. It's not your night for chores and yet—

Did you know that there is a difference between doing what is **expected** of you and **giving** freely of yourself? The Bible tells us we are to be obedient servants of God:

"Live as servants of God."

—1 Peter 2:16 (NIV)

God's chosen ones, such as Moses, Abraham and Jacob, were obedient servants. Sometimes they questioned or doubted until God reassured them and promised them great blessings. At other times, they were quick to obey. In those times of quick obedience, they set a good example for us to follow.

When God called Mary, she did not doubt or wrestle with His choices—**Mary gave!** She gave up herself to the Lord in complete faith when she said,

"I am the Lord's servant"

—Luke 1:38 (NIV)

As you walk through your day surrounded by God's blessings, look for ways to give of your love! Whether it is a chat with a lonely neighbor, baking cookies for a sick friend, or doing your chores for a smile instead of money, know that your giving heart is a blessed gift to God!

Now, about those dishes—

For You to Do:

Cut apart word cards.
Match and glue to the boxes below.

God | for | loves | a | giver. | cheerful
2 Corinthians 9:7

Mary's Daily Maze

To find out what Mary did each day, follow her through the maze.

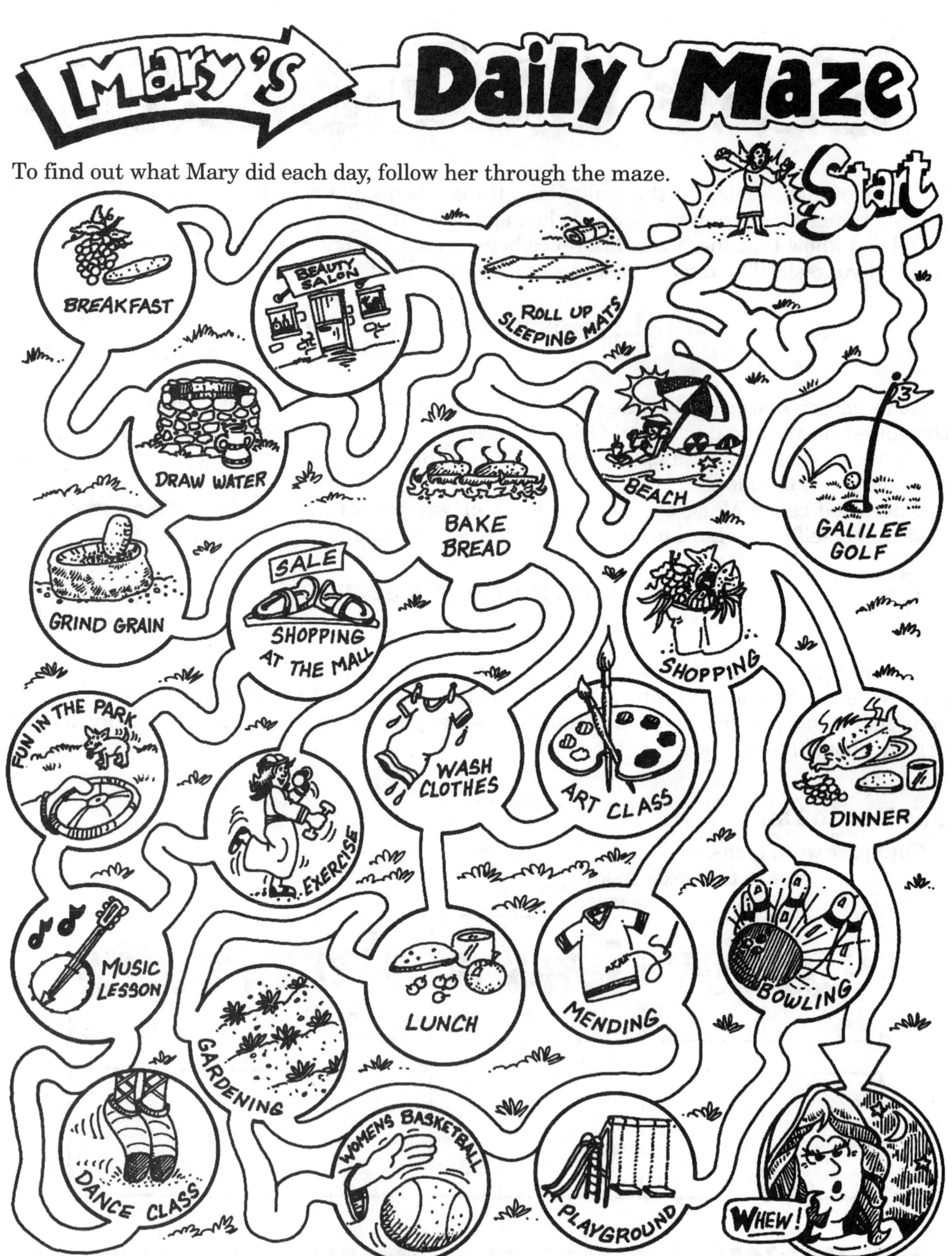

The Bible tells of many different shrubs and flowers, from myrrh to roses. One of the prettiest and most often mentioned flowers in Scripture is the lily. The lily we are most familiar with is the Easter lily. It is noted for its beautiful white petals and sweet scent. This snowy flower has become a symbol of purity. Many artists have painted Mary surrounded by lilies to remind us of her purity of heart and soul before God.

Mary was a virgin when the angel told her she would be the mother of God's Son and even when Jesus was born. That was a miracle intended to reveal God's power. It also proves that Mary had a gentle purity, a clean, fresh heart and spirit. A lily is much the same: a gentle blossom of pure whiteness, delicate and sweet scented among all the flowers of the garden.

Mary was like a lily among thorns, blessed among all women (Luke 1:42). Mary's heart was pure and faithfully devoted to God. He saw in her a fresh purity and whiteness of spirit.

> "We show that we are servants of God by living a pure life."
> —2 Corinthians 6:6 (ICB)

Lilies grow wild in many parts of the world in soil that is sandy and not too damp. Grown from scaly bulbs, lilies send forth bright green stems that hold clusters of trumpet-shaped flowers. Their beauty is so breathtaking that Jesus said not even a king in all his fine robes and riches can compare to the God gifted beauty of lilies in the field (Matthew 6:28, 29; and Luke 12:27, 28). And if you have ever smelled a lily, you'll know why the oil of these special flowers was treasured for perfumes in Biblical days.

Lilies are a treat for the senses—from sight to smell, from blossom to flower, they are beauty only a loving God could create! God even tells us His love is like a lily; that as this gentle flower blooms into extraordinary beauty, so shall His love bloom for us!

> "[My love] . . . will blossom like a lily" (Hosea 14:5, ICB).

Why can't lilies talk? To find out, use the code at the right to decode the message below.

What would it have been like to have dinner at Mary's house? These activities will help you find out. In Mary's time, people often sat on mats on the floor while they ate.

Make a Mat

Needed
- large colored sheets of (18 x 12) construction paper
- 2 x 10 inch strips of construction paper (8 per mat)
- scissors, glue

Directions
- Draw a one inch margin on the sides of the mat
- Make 5 vertical slits 2 inches wide in the sheet of paper inside the margins of the mat
- Weave the first strip into the mat in an under/over fashion; the next strip weave over/under, etc.
- Glue strip ends to mat after weaving

Make a Meal

Teachers should select items from the list for children to taste.

Mary's Menu
- Bread (use pancakes or tortillas)
- Lentils (beans—raw or cooked)
- Nuts (hazel, pistachio, almond)
- Eggs (usually boiled)
- Fish (sardines are similar to what she used)
- Kefir (similar to plain yogurt)
- Vegetables (lettuce, beets, cucumbers, olives)
- Fruit (figs, dates, grapes, mulberries, pomegranates)
- Melon (Cantalope, watermelon)
- Drink (lots of water)

Preparing the Food
- The first job to be done was making bread.
  Children can make pancakes on a griddle or warm tortillas on a hot plate.
- Next, the fruit and vegetables were washed, cut up (if necessary) and placed in bowls.
- Foods to be tasted should be arranged on a table.
- Mats made earlier will be used for sitting.
- Sandals and headdresses from "What was in Back Then" (page 15) may be worn for the meal.

Handwashing
Before the meal, the people washed their hands. This was done in a special way. Friends and family members helped each other by pouring water over each others' hands, one hand at a time, 1/2 cup per hand, allowing the water to run from the finger tips to the wrist and then turning their hands over so the water ran back down their fingertips and into a basin.

Prayer
Prayer was said before each meal. A common prayer was "Blessed are Thou, Jehovah, our God, King of the world, Who causes to come forth bread from the earth."

The Meal
Not all the items listed were served at every meal. Breakfast consisted of bread and fruit. At midday, bread, kefir, vegetables, fruit, and nuts were often served. The main meal was in the evening. Bread, lentils, fish, eggs, kefir, and vegetables were served. This meal was a time of family visiting and sharing.

Bread was the main item for each meal. Silverware was not used; bread was used as a spoon to dip into cooked lentil or kefir. Otherwise, fingers were used. Eating from a common dish was a sign of friendship.

Prayer
A prayer of thanksgiving followed the meal.

Handwashing
After each meal, the people washed their hands again using the same method as before.

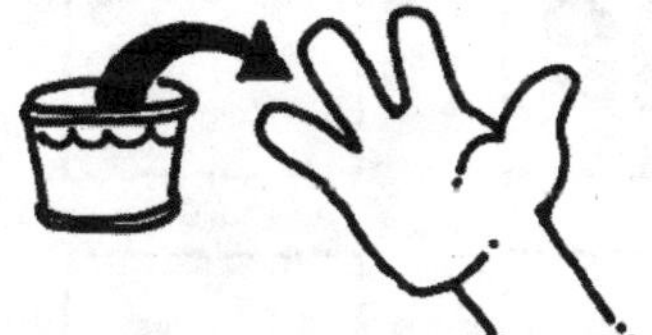  

If we live a faithful, loving, honest life and keep our hearts pure before God, we will behold a **glorious** sight!

Cut out each square at the bottom of the page (one square at a time).

Glue the square into its corresponding box on the grid.

When you are finished, you will see why a pure heart is truly a blessing!

	A	B	C	D
1	A1	B1	C1	D1
2	A2	B2	C2	D2
3	A3	B3	C3	D3
4	A4	B4	C4	D4
5	A5	B5	C5	D5

Matthew 5:8

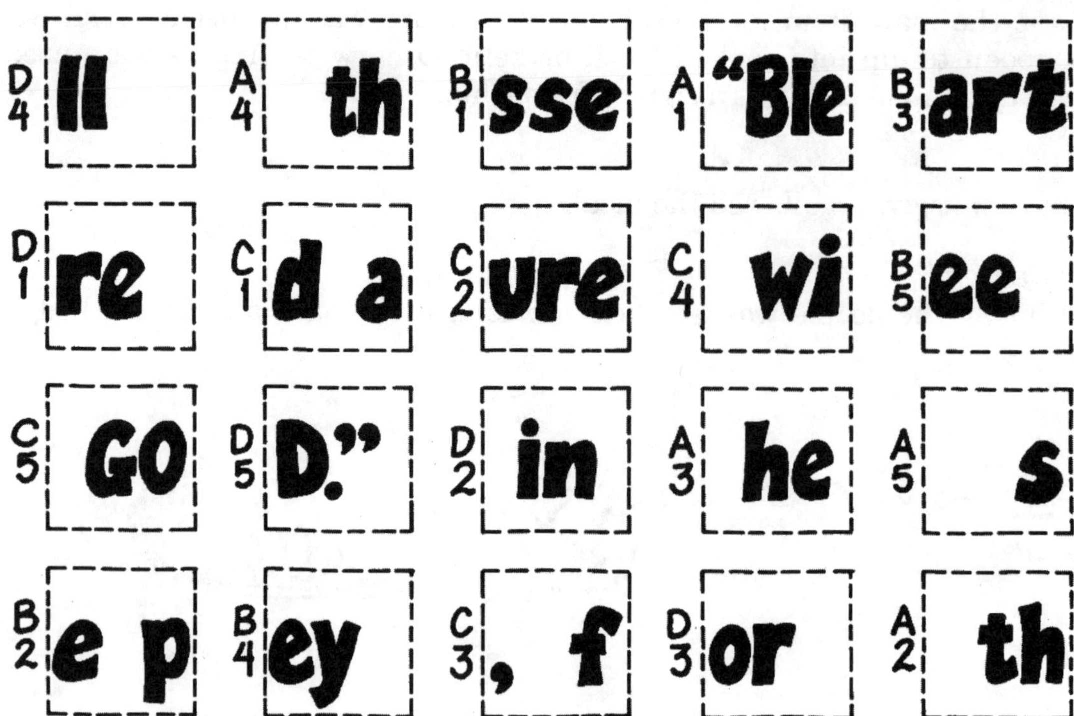

What Was IN Back Then

Jeans and tennis shoes hadn't been invented yet. At least another 1800 years would pass before zippers would be used. Buttons were available only for the wealthy people. What did the people wear in Mary's time?

What was in back then?

Would you believe T-shirts and sandals?

Something like a long T-shirt was worn by the men and women. Over this, they wore an outer tunic (shirt) or dress that came to their knees. Over this, they wore a cloak, kind of like a long jacket, which was belted in at the waist. On their heads, they wore a headdress made of a square of cloth (about 2' x 2') with a headband to hold it in place. The people loved to wear bright colors (blues, purples, reds). On their feet, they wore sandals made of wood or leather in warm weather and boots in the winter.

Make Your Own Sandals

Needed: corrugated cardboard, yarn, scissors, paper

Directions: Make patterns by tracing the feet of the child; enlarge the patterns by 1/2 inch all the way around. Use the patterns to make two sandals of cardboard. Using the diagram below as a guide, punch small holes in the cardboard. Lace the yarn through the cardboard as shown.

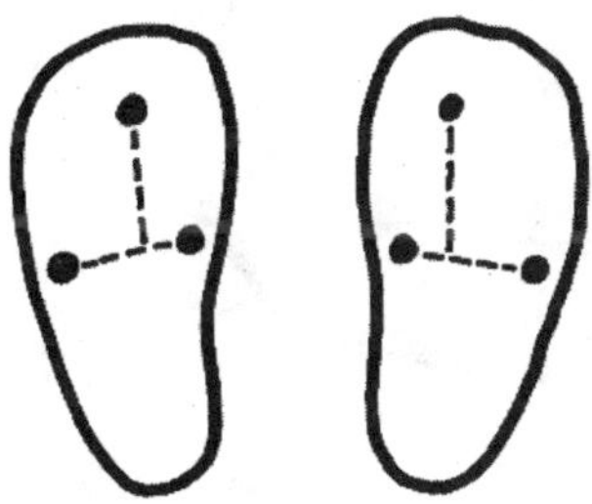

Make Your Own Headdress

Needed: a 2' x 2' cloth for each child; yarn for headband; markers to decorate cloth

Directions: Children may draw stripes on the cloth in bright colors. To make headband, twist together or loosely weave 6 two foot lengths of yarn and knot the ends.

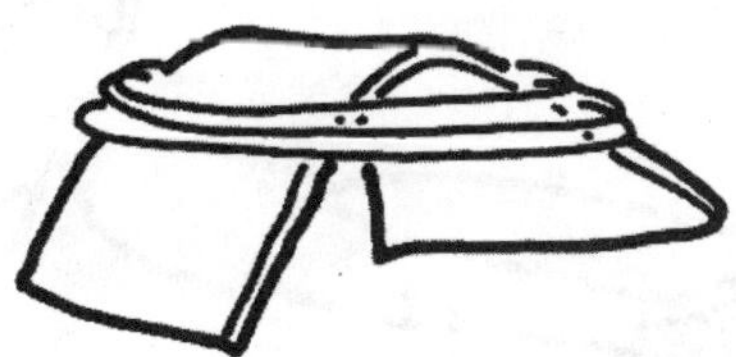

What Was In Back Then?

Color and put together these people who wore what was "in back then."

Scripture Memory

Mercy Flower

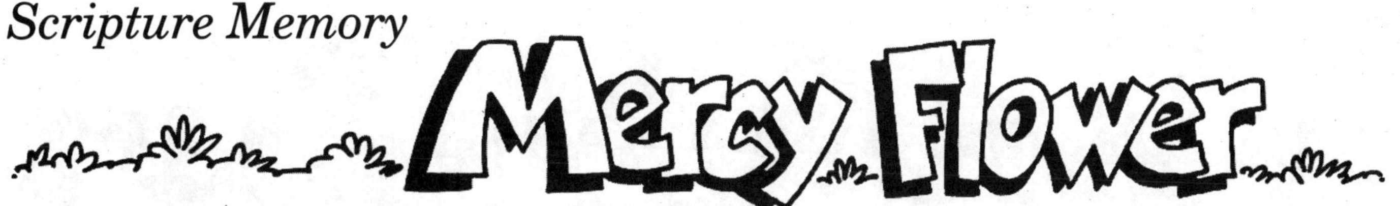

"God will always give mercy to those who worship him."
—Luke 1:50 (ICB)

Mary learned about God's mercy when He chose her to be the mother of Jesus!

God's mercy is like a beautiful flower; bright, alive and waiting for us to pick it for our own!

To help you memorize this Scripture verse, make the Mercy Flower by coloring and cutting out the petals below and gluing them to the outline by matching the numbers on the petals!

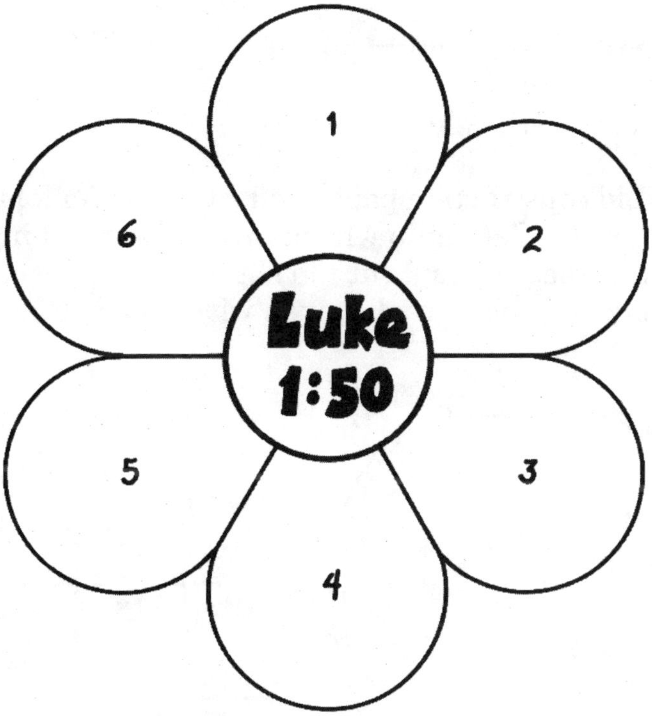

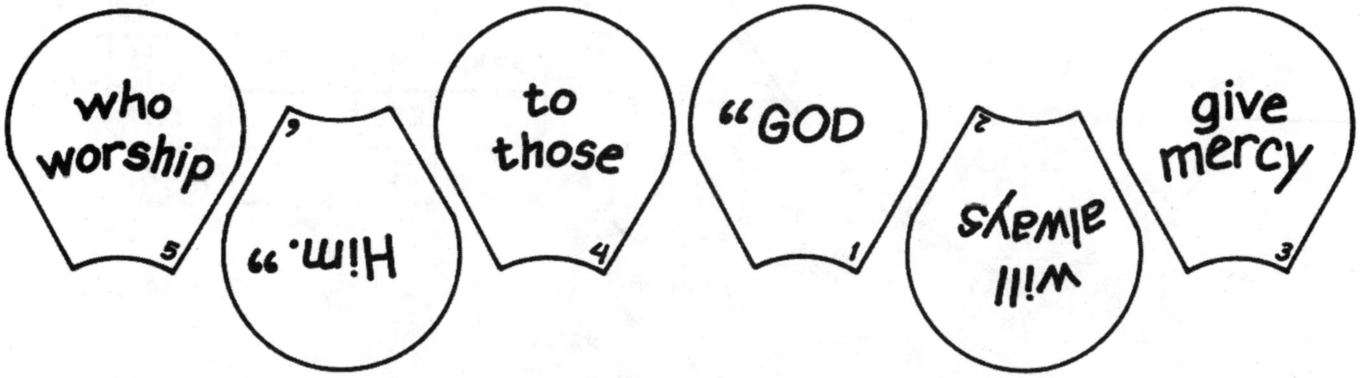

Hide It In Your Heart

"My soul praises the Lord;
my heart is happy because God is my Savior.
I am not important, but God has shown his
care for me, his servant girl."
Luke 1:46-48 (ICB)

Mary remembered God's words to her by storing them in her heart. To help you to remember to store God's word in your heart, complete the art project below.

Needed: red construction paper
1 safety pin for each heart
copies of the Scripture puzzle
scissors and glue
heart pattern below

Directions: Fold construction paper and cut heart on fold. Glue scripture puzzle to the inside. Cut tab on front cover by trimming the tip of the heart as shown in diagram and cut tab slit on puzzle page.
To solve the puzzle, color in all boxes with words that begin with the letters D, K, R, or W.

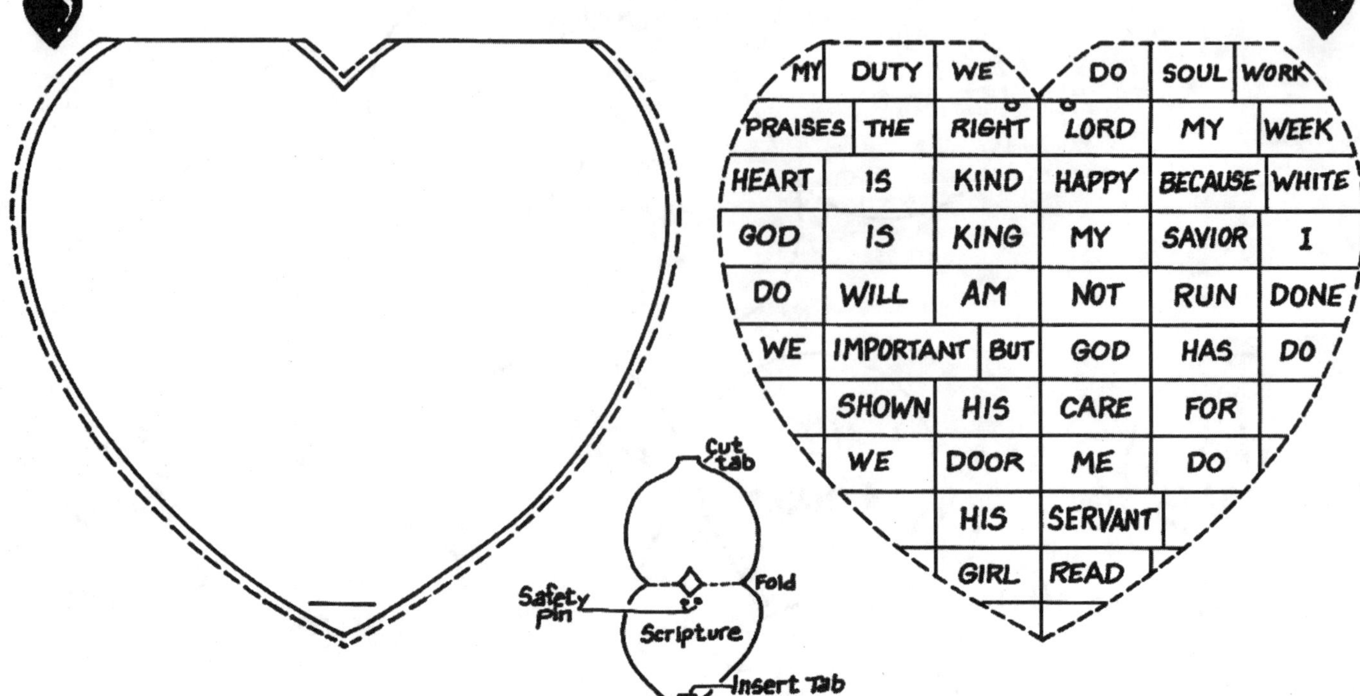

MY	DUTY	WE	DO	SOUL	WORK
PRAISES	THE	RIGHT	LORD	MY	WEEK
HEART	IS	KIND	HAPPY	BECAUSE	WHITE
GOD	IS	KING	MY	SAVIOR	I
DO	WILL	AM	NOT	RUN	DONE
WE	IMPORTANT	BUT	GOD	HAS	DO
	SHOWN	HIS	CARE	FOR	
	WE	DOOR	ME	DO	
		HIS	SERVANT		
		GIRL	READ		

Precious Parents

Whose face is shining when the day is new
And sings good morning just to you?
Whose hands tuck you to sleep each night
And hold your heart as stars shine bright?

A tough riddle? Not really, if you think for a moment about whom you begin and end each day with in your home—your MOTHER and FATHER!

What a precious, holy gift God has given us in a mother's and father's love! We can learn so much about how God loves us by taking a look at how our own parents love their children.

Our Mothers and Fathers love us enough to *provide* for us; wanting to give us all things good and beautiful. They *protect* us, carefully watching where we go and what we do so that we do not get hurt. Our parents *teach* us right from wrong, when to say yes and when to say no. They help us learn to be whole people, with hearts that love and minds that think!

Mothers and fathers are God's gift to us. We see and feel their love in so many ways! If we are so strongly loved by parents, think how much more our Heavenly Father loves each of us—His children!

"How great is the love the Father has lavished on us, that we should be called children of God!" (1 John 3:1).

Parent Proverbs

The book of Proverbs has much to teach us about loving and respecting parents. Use your Bible (ICB) and the book of Proverbs to find the missing words in the Scripture verses below. (The reference is given for each one.)

1. "Children are _______ of their parents" (17:6).
2. "Make your father and mother _______" (23:25).
3. "Don't _____ _____ of your father" (30:17).
4. "Don't refuse to _______ your mother" (30:17).
5. "_____ to your father's teaching and do not ______ your mother's advice" (1:8).
6. "Their teaching will _______ your life" (1:9).

Now see if you can fit each word you found into the hearts!

When Mary Said "NO"

Mary taught Jesus
all that she knew
of God's love and wisdom—
of His promises true.

From her He learned kindness
toward others to show;
in her He saw gentleness,
peace, and love flow.

But, what did Jesus do
when Mary said "No"?
Did He shake His head,
turn to go?

Did He disobey
to get His way?

To find out what Jesus did when Mary said "No," decode the puzzle below by coloring in all the spaces marked with dots (•). Then read the words you have colored. Check your answer in Luke 2:51.

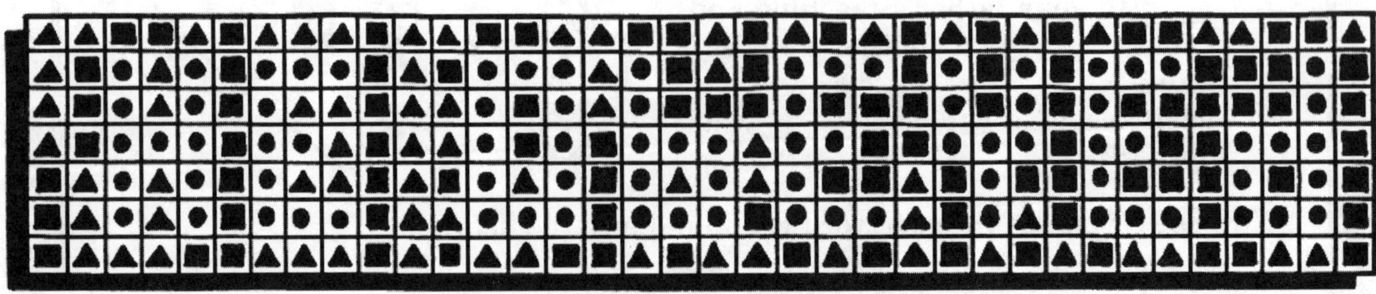

Mary's Puzzle Peace

- Cut out puzzle and pieces below.
- Reassemble and glue to a sheet of construction paper.
- Color your puzzle.

Getting a Rise Out of Yeast

(The science of bread making)

Bread was the main food in Mary's day, so she must have made a lot of it. Although there are many different kinds of bread and methods of preparing it and baking it have changed since her day, bread is still basically the same. It is also fun to make!

One of the most important ingredients in bread is yeast. Yeast is also called *leavening* in the Bible. Yeast is everywhere—even floating in the air! Yeast is made up of tiny plants called yeasts. Yeasts bud and form more yeasts. This happens very fast!

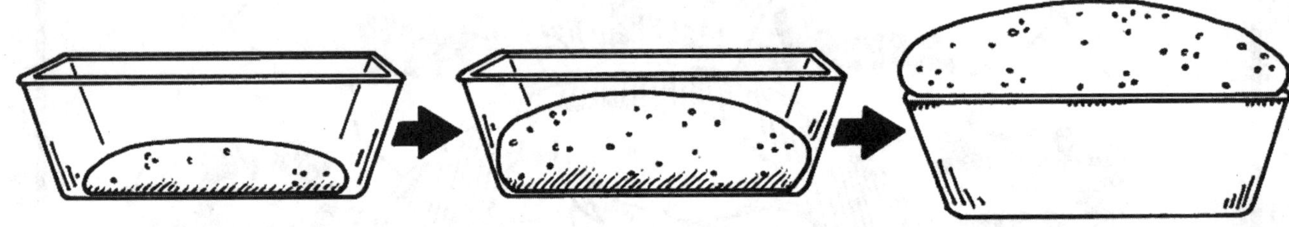

When yeast is put in flour, sugar, and water, a chemical change takes place. The yeasts attack the flour, changing it to sugar. Then they change the sugar to alcohol and carbon dioxide gas. This is important to bread making. As the gas bubbles throughout the dough, it makes the bread raise, or grow in size, and it makes the bread lighter. The Egyptians were the first to discover this way of making bread.

Bread made without yeast was used for holy celebrations. Mary made this "unleavened bread" for feasts such as Passover (Exodus 12:14-17).

Try This

To see how leaven works, make pancakes and watch them as they cook on the griddle. As they cook, bubbles come to the top. Do you remember what makes the bubbles?

Each day, Mary went to the well to draw water. Some wells were public wells and the water was free. Other wells were owned and the water was sold. Carrying the water in a large jar balanced on top of her head, Mary would take it home for use in cooking, drinking, and washing.

What Is a Well?

A well is a hole in the ground that goes down to an underground stream or to pockets of water trapped between layers of rock. Long ago, these holes had to be dug by hand. Once the hole was dug, it was lined with rocks or bricks to keep the sides of the well from caving in. Water usually had to be drawn from a dug well with buckets. (Today, most wells are drilled and a metal pipe is pushed into the ground. Then a pump is attached to draw the water out.) Some wells deliver the water on their own. These are "artesian wells." In an artesian well, the water source underground is connected to a body of water somewhere higher than the ground where the well was dug or drilled, like a mountain lake. The water from the higher source creates pressure on the water in the underground stream and pushes the water up into the well. To see how this works, try this experiment:

Needed: 2 plastic straws
1 rubber band
1 medium balloon
water and a bowl
glue

Directions:

Cut a small hole in one side of a straw.

Cut the other straw into a two-inch piece.

Insert this piece into the first straw.

Press the straw in far enough to hold but not so far as to block water flow. Seal with glue.

This short straw represents an artesian well.

Fill a balloon with water and place the mouth of the balloon over the end of the long straw. Wrap a rubber band around to secure.

Allow one child to hold the straws, covering the open end of the long straw with his finger.

Another child may hold the balloon. A third child may hold the bowl under the straw to catch the water.

Direct the child holding the balloon to gently squeeze the balloon, forcing the water into the straw and up the well. Or simply raise the balloon so it is higher than the top of the well. The water should naturally flow out of the well.

To make Mary's well, color the water blue and then color the well. Cut out both pieces, being careful not to cut off the tabs. Carefully follow the directions for cutting the top of the well. Glue the sides of the well together. Fold the tabs on water down. Push the water into the well from the bottom and glue the tabs.

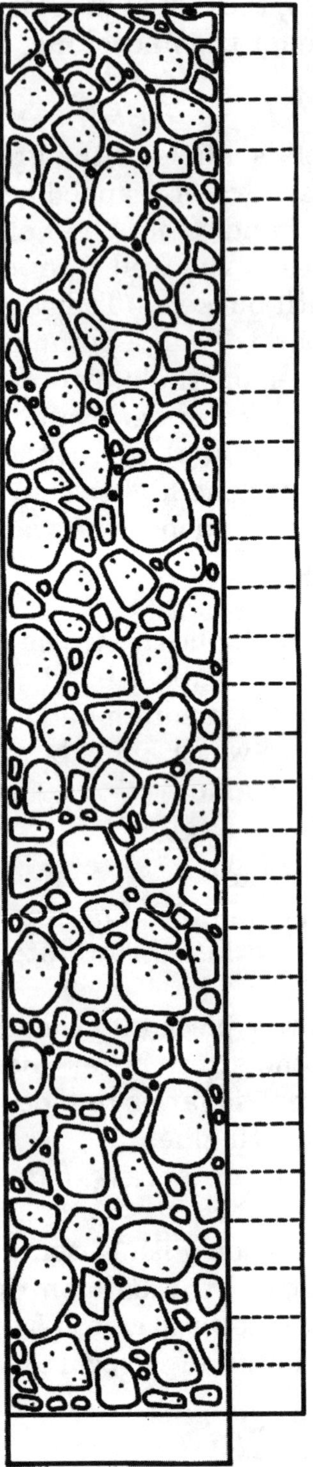

Mary's House

Mary's house probably had only one room. Made of clay brick, the house had a flat roof and a packed dirt floor. In warm weather, the family slept on the roof. Work was also done there. The door to the house may have been a curtain of cloth.

Directions:
- Cut out the house.
- Fold on the bold vertical lines.
- Glue flap to the back of the door section.
- Cut out roof, be sure to cut around tabs.
- Fold tabs down and glue roof to house 1/2 inch down from top.
- Cut around the ladder.
- Fold tabs so that ladder will fit on to side of house.
- Glue tabs to inside of house wall.

A village may be made by making many houses and using the well from page 24.

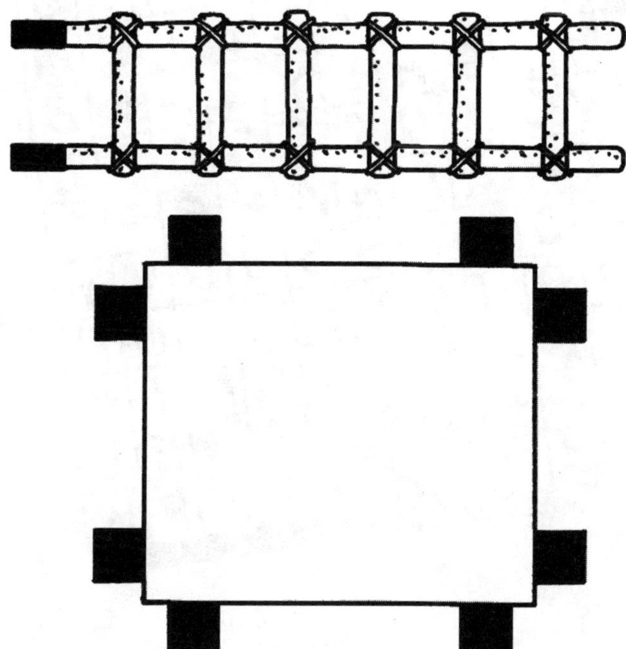

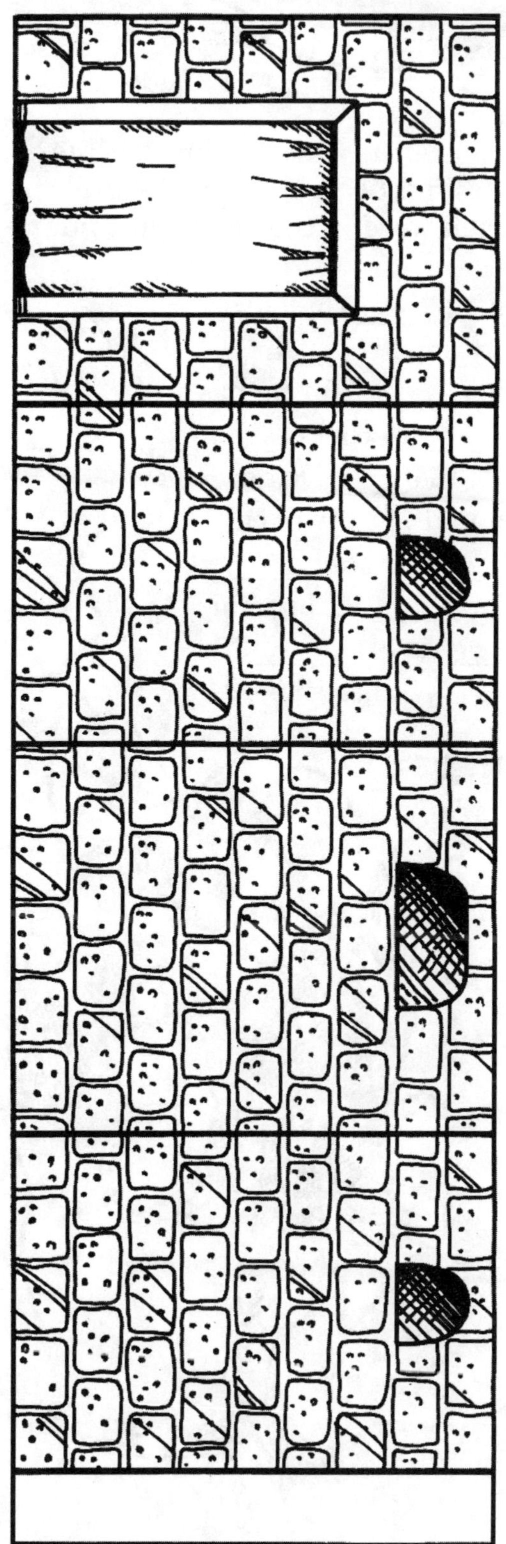

SEEK and You Shall Find

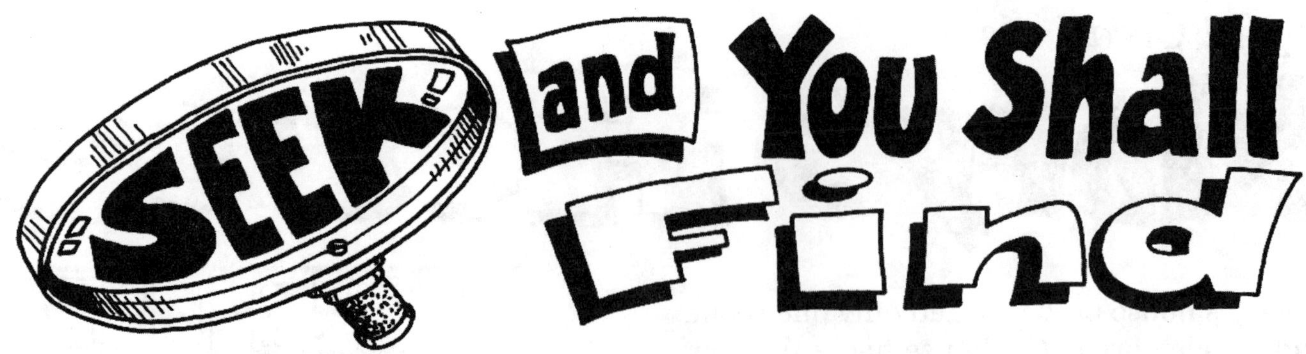

Here are the first few lines of Mary's song, called the "Magnificat," but some of the words are missing! Look in your NIV Bible at Luke 1:46-49 and fill in the blanks. Now see if you can find each word in the word hunt puzzle below!

"My soul _____ the Lord
and my spirit _____ in
God my ______, for he has
been _____ of the _____
state of his _____. From
now on all _____ will call
me _____, for the _____
has done _____ things for
me-_____ is his ______."
Luke 1:46-49

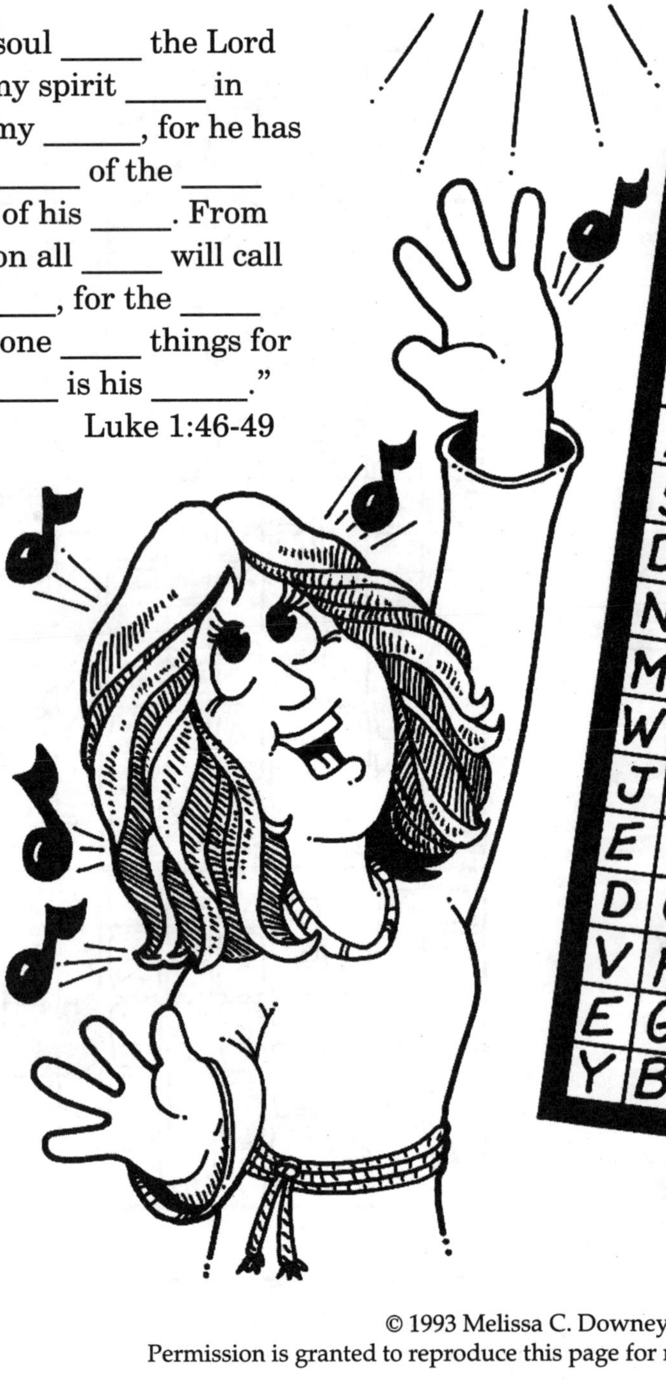

J	S	E	R	M	L	E	N	V	T
E	G	R	E	A	T	E	R	P	A
N	A	O	J	O	I	T	L	M	L
G	G	L	O	R	I	F	I	E	S
T	E	S	I	M	N	E	S	A	T
Y	N	D	C	A	N	O	V	S	H
A	E	R	E	Y	P	I	R	T	N
S	R	G	S	F	O	N	K	A	H
D	A	R	E	R	D	E	M	C	U
N	T	I	V	E	L	E	I	L	M
M	I	G	H	T	Y	O	N	E	B
W	O	I	O	L	E	B	D	B	L
J	N	A	L	N	A	E	F	G	E
E	S	H	Y	B	S	H	U	V	Y
D	O	H	L	S	E	R	L	O	P
V	F	S	E	R	V	A	N	T	M
E	G	L	Q	B	S	S	D	E	L
Y	B	V	C	H	O	P	M	R	B

Match the symbols on the map with the symbols and names on this page.
Write the name of the place in the space.

●   Nazareth

    Jerusalem

★   Bethlehem

    Sea of Galilee

▲   Egypt

∼   Jordan River

    Great Sea

▬   Dead Sea

The shaded area on the map represents mountains.

Now you are ready to map Mary's miles.
1. Begin at Nazareth. Using a red map pencil or pen, draw a line to Bethlehem (75 miles) where Jesus was born.
2. Next, draw a line from Bethlehem to Jerusalem (5 miles) where she met Simeon and Anna in the temple.
3. From Jerusalem draw a line back to Bethlehem (5 miles).
4. Then draw a line down and across to Egypt (120 miles).
5. Do you remember where she traveled next? Yes, all the way back to Nazareth (195 miles)!

How many miles did she travel? $75+5+5+120+195=$ _______!

Remember that to travel these many miles, Mary rode a donkey or walked!

Use your map to answer these questions.

1. What town is nearest the Sea of Galilee?

____

2. What two cities are in Judea?

_____________ and _____________

3. Is Galilee north or south of Samaria?

____

4. Is Samaria north or south of Judea?

____

5. Is Egypt east or west of Judea?

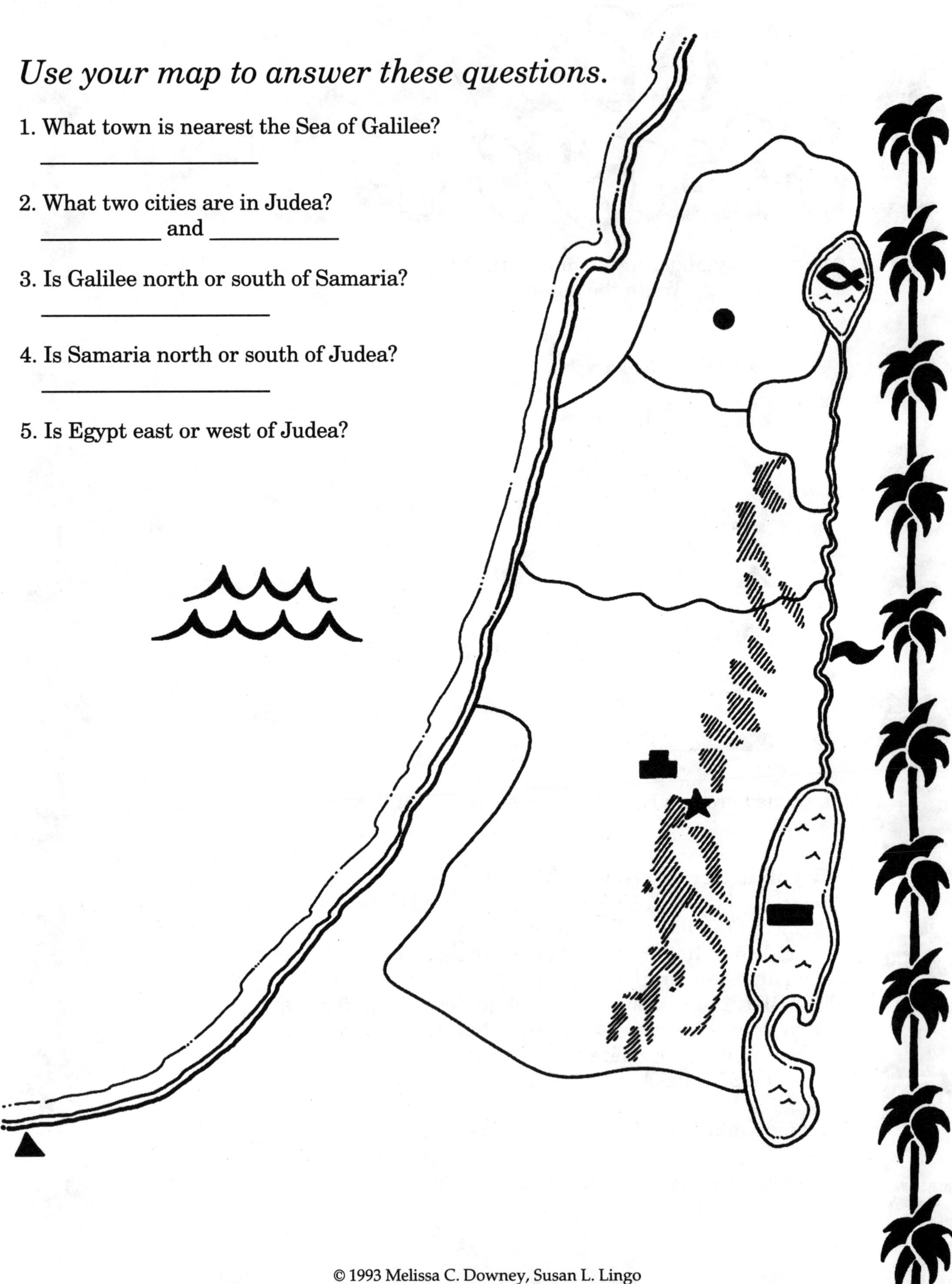

Have you ever felt a hard job was not possible? Have you ever cried out, "That can't be"?

Is anything truly impossible? Use the code at the right to decode the message below.

A B C D E F G H I J K L
M N O P Q R S T U V
W X Y Z

"_______________ ______________

_______________ ______________

_______________ ______________."

Luke 1:37

Now unscramble the circled letters above to find the missing word below!

With God, all things are possible
and our hearts are filled with __ __ __ __!

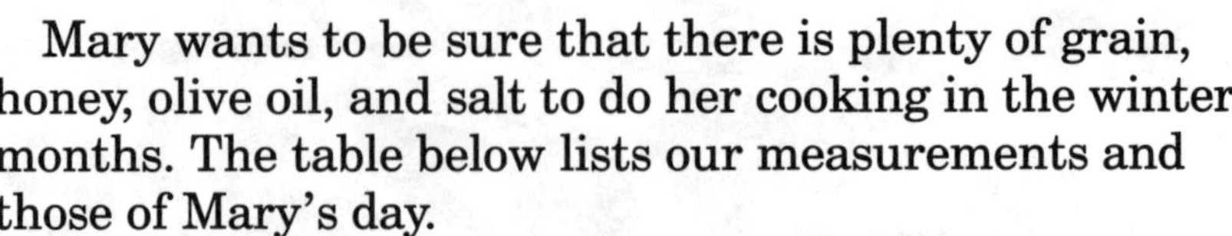

Mary wants to be sure that there is plenty of grain, honey, olive oil, and salt to do her cooking in the winter months. The table below lists our measurements and those of Mary's day.

Dry Measure

Our Measures	Mary's Measures
20 quarts	1 ephah
7 quarts	1 seah
2 quarts	1 omer
1 quart	1 cab

Liquid Measure

Our Measures	Mary's Measures
6 gallons	1 bath
4 quarts	1 hin

Can you figure out how much of each item Mary needs by changing Mary's measures to ours? You will use multiplication to do this. For example, if Mary needs 4 ephahs of wheat you would do this:

$$1 \text{ ephah} = 20 \text{ quarts}$$
$$4 \text{ ephahs} \times 20 \text{ quarts} = 80 \text{ quarts}$$
$$4 \times 20 = 80$$

Mary would need 80 quarts of wheat.

Our Measures	Mary's Measures
80 quarts, wheat (20 x 4 = 80)	4 ephahs, wheat
___ quarts, barley (7 x 6 = ___)	6 seahs, barley
___ quarts, salt (2 x 3 = ___)	3 omers, salt
___ quarts, rye (1 x 1 1/2 = ___)	1 1/2 cabs, rye

Now, let's do division. Change our measurements into Mary's.

36 gallons, oil (36 ÷ 6 = ___)	___baths, oil
16 quarts, honey (16 ÷ 4 = ___)	___ hins, honey

The 5th Is the 1st

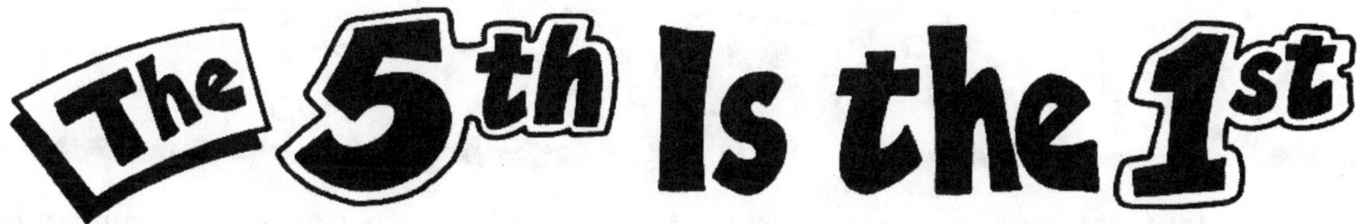

When Moses stood on the slopes of Mt. Sinai, God gave him two holy stone tablets on which His finger had written the Ten Commandments. When God gave us the FIFTH commandment, it was really the FIRST! Read Ephesians 6:1-3. Here we are reminded that Commandment 5 was the FIRST commandment with a promise: God has promised us a long, joyous life if we keep this important Commandment!

In the puzzle below, you will find God's 5th (and 1st!) Commandment. Begin at the arrow and skip every other letter a you read around the heart *twice*. Write the letters in the blanks. (We've given you the first and last letters!)

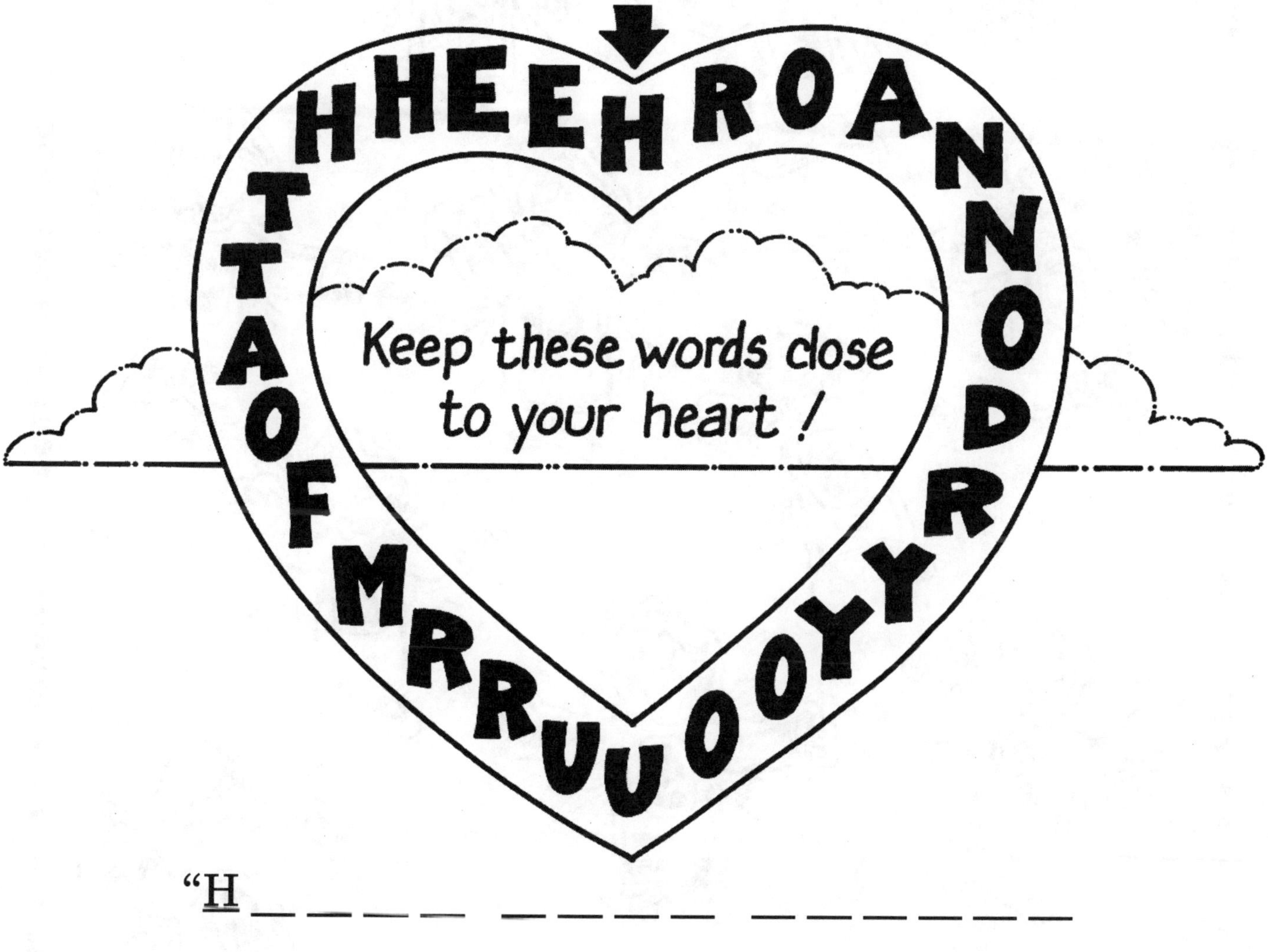

"H_ _ _ _ _ _ _ _ _ _ _ _ _ _ _ _ _ _

_ _ _ _ _ _ _ _ _ _ _ _ _ _ R."

—Deuteronomy 5:16 (ICB)

What An Angel

Circle the 7 identical angels and unscramble their letters to name the angel who visited Mary. The remaining angels will tell you the name of the special baby born to Mary. Write their names on the spaces at the bottom of the page.

The angel's name was: _______________________

The special baby's name was: _______________